On Consciousness

Ted Honderich

University of Pittsburgh Press

© Ted Honderich, 2004

Published in the United States by the
University of Pittsburgh Press, Pittsburgh, Pa., 15260

First published in the UK by
Edinburgh University Press

ISBN 0-8229-4245-3

A CIP record for this book is available from the
Library of Congress.